FROM RHYME TO READING:

HOW LANGUAGE PLAY BUILDS TO LITERACY

A Parent's Guide *by Literacy Educator*

Dr Marion Milton

First Published by Literacy Pathways Press

Copyright © 2025 Dr Marion Milton

ISBN

Paperback 978-1-7642901-0-4

E-book   978-1-7642901-1-1

Dr Marion Milton is the author of this work and claims copyright under the Copyright Act. The information in this text is based on the author's many years of experience and research in the field.

All rights reserved. Apart from any fair dealing for the purpose of private study, research, criticism or review permitted under the Copyright act, no part of this publication may be reproduced, stored in a retrieval system or transmitted, in any means, electronic, mechanical, photocopying, recording or otherwise without prior written permission of the author. Enquiries to be made through the publisher.

Cover Design: Haseeb Ahmed.

Editor: Marion Milton

Literacy Pathways Press

Perth, Western Australia, 6000.

www.literacypathways.com

info@literacypathways.com

CONTENTS

INTRODUCTION 4

CHAPTER 1: HOW CAN I ASSIST MY CHILD'S LANGUAGE DEVELOPMENT? 8

CHAPTER 2: HOW CAN I MAKE MY CHILD'S WORLD RICHER AND MAKE IT FUN? ...16

CHAPTER 3: HOW CAN I CREATE A LANGUAGE RICH WORLD? 24

CHAPTER 4: HOW DO WE LEARN TO SPEAK? 32

CHAPTER 5: HOW CAN I BE A LANGUAGE MODEL? 43

CHAPTER 6: HOW CAN I ENRICH MY CHILD'S VOCABULARY? 48

CHAPTER 7: LET'S ALL SING! 55

CHAPTER 8: LET'S PLAY LANGUAGE GAMES 65

CHAPTER 9: LET'S READ TOGETHER 72

CHAPTER 10: LET'S SCRIBBLE, WRITE, TYPE AND DRAW! 87

CHAPTER 11: LET'S GET READY FOR KINDY 91

CHAPTER 12: LET'S START SCHOOL! 94

ABOUT THE AUTHOR 100

INTRODUCTION

Congratulations on choosing this book about helping your child to develop his or her language and pre-literacy skills before school begins. It shows your interest and concern for your child's future formal education. Following the activities in this book are some of the first steps towards helping your child to become a successful reader and writer.

As a former classroom teacher, I gained experience in teaching children from their first year through to all levels in primary school and early secondary school. I was always fascinated with how children learn to read and so went on to further study. I became a Doctor of Education, specialising in the psycholinguistic processes of early language development and its relationship to beginning reading. For many years I instructed pre-service teachers on how to teach reading and writing to young children. Part of this was how to recognise and assist children experiencing literacy difficulties, as well as how to develop the English skills of children from other language backgrounds.

Over the years I spent a lot of time in schools observing teachers working with children learning literacy, as well as conducting research in schools to find the best ways to teach for early success. Early childhood teachers understand that a child with well-developed language skills will be prepared to learn to read and for other learning that takes place in the classroom.

INTRODUCTION

This book will help you ensure your child is ready to learn to read and write when they* start school. The path is through learning nursery rhymes, playing language games and building their understanding and use of language. You, the parent, are crucial as your child's first teacher. A child who knows lots of words, is curious about their world, asks questions and likes to listen to stories, is already developing important skills. Those children will find it much easier to become literate than children with no early preparation. Before I go on to tell you the about the activities and games that will help, I will briefly talk about why I wrote this book and some of the information about learning to read and write in English.

While out in schools talking with teachers, many confirmed my own experience, that some children come to school with insufficient language skills to be able to cope with the literacy demands of the classroom. They also noted that a growing number of **parents wanted more knowledge about what they could do at home to help. I had spent many years teaching pre-service teachers and running workshops for classroom teachers, but I had only given a few talks to parents.

For the last ten years I was a Consultant School Reviewer for public and private education systems in Western Australia (2014 to 2024). As part of those reviews, I spoke with parent groups about their children's education. Some of the statements and questions they asked, highlighted the fact that many, while interested and concerned, did not know the best ways to help prepare or support their children's learning prior to school entry and then how to continue to support them as they advanced through the school years.

The idea to write books for parents began to germinate. I had written many articles, research reports and book chapters for teachers and teacher-education students, but none for parents. Educators and

Education systems have increased their focus on pre-school education and the importance of a good start. The time had come to write books for parents that I hope will not only give you a greater understanding of how children learn to read but give you a few ideas to help prepare and support your children for school literacy learning.

So here is the first book that aims to give you, the parent, the understanding and confidence to develop your child's language and pre-literacy skills. I do not want this book to be an academic tome, so I have limited the research studies I mention to seminal or groundbreaking research that has changed the way we think about learning to be literate. Sufficient information is given about the research studies mentioned for an interested person to find them.

There are a series of podcasts following the same theme. To listen to the podcasts go to: *From Rhyme to Reading* and Beyond by Dr Marion Milton. A follow-up book, (*A Good Start to Reading*) for parents of children in the first years of school, is on the way.

*NOTE: Rather than write out 'his or her' each time, I have followed the convention of using 'they', even when talking about 'your child'.

**NOTE: In the following pages I will use the word 'parents' to include grandparents and carers.

NOTE

When you read this book, you can choose to read it straight through from beginning to end in order. If, however, you feel you have a general understanding of particular sections, and already know enough about some areas, you can skip those sections. Alternatively, you can go directly to the tips and activities in each chapter.

CHAPTER 1

HOW CAN I ASSIST MY CHILD'S LANGUAGE DEVELOPMENT?

This book will help you ensure your child is ready to take on the task of learning to read and write when they start school. I mentioned earlier that learning to read and write is not the same as learning to talk. Children are 'pre-programmed' to learn to speak the language they are born into, but the same is not so for reading and writing.

Talking and Reading

We will look into this more deeply later, but a brief explanation is that humans first began to write about 5000 years ago, far fewer than the 300,000 years Homo Sapiens have been on earth. When we speak, words blur together, our intonation patterns do not have a break between each word. Try saying *Mum and Dad*. Notice that it sounds like *Mumnd Dad*. We do not clearly separate out *Mum – and – Dad*. When we learn to speak, we understand the meaning, but do not clearly separate the words. It is different for reading and writing. We not only have to separate the words, but we need to break them down into letters and sounds. Reading and writing do not come naturally to us. Literacy skills have to be taught.

Not many years ago, this became a revolutionary idea. At that time, teachers had been erroneously taught that learning to read and write was just like learning to speak. They thought that all teachers had to do was to expose children to good books and encourage them to write and it would all happen naturally. It was called the 'Whole Language' approach. For a few bright children this approach was fairly successful.

When some children did not pick up reading and writing skills easily, the fault was often placed within the child, in other words it was thought that the child was deficient in some way. If those children were lucky, they then received remedial reading lessons and were able to catch up to their classmates.

Does it Matter?

Unfortunately, the assumptions about how we learn to read and write were based on faulty research, undertaken back in the early 1970s. Newer and ongoing research, has demonstrated that most children need to be taught the letters and sounds (called Phonics) in order to learn to read. Most grandparents would have been taught to read by learning the alphabet first, then learning simple words, and putting them together in sentences. Due to the problems some children faced when taught that way, the oversimplified reading materials, and the fact that it was a very slow method of teaching children to read, research was conducted to try to find a better way. The research done in the 1970s that led to the Whole Language movement, focused on the overall aim of reading, that is to gain meaning from text.

To that end, a benefit did arise from the movement by the insistence that children deserved to read quality children's literature. Unfortunately, that positive focus on good books lead to a de-emphasis on phonics, and at least 20 percent of children failed to learn to read. Those children then needed remedial reading lessons. The Whole language method lasted for decades until more scientific research was done in the early 2000s.

Some of that research looked at what we need to do to read. A simplified version of what we need to do is that, to become readers we have to do two main things. We have to be able get the words off the page and then we have to understand what those words mean in a phrase or sentences. We cannot make meaning, if we are unable decipher the letters that make words. It seemed that we did need to teach children phonics (the letter sound relationships in words), but we did not want to go back to the way our grandparents were taught.

What do we Now Know about Reading?

Groundbreaking research was undertaken in the UK that investigated how Phonics were taught in England and Scotland. In 2005 a report on the findings of the 7 year study by Johnston and Watson was published (Scottish Executive Education Department). In England a traditional method of teaching phonics was used, by teaching all of the alphabet first and then teaching children how to sound out words and read simple books. Children did not start to learn how to blend sounds together to make new words until the start of their second year of school.

That method was compared with how the Scottish schools in the study taught Phonics. They taught the same things but in a different way and different order. The researchers called this method *Synthetic Phonics*. Teachers taught children only a few of the most common letter-sound combinations first and then taught them to blend the sounds to make words, and to break words apart by sounding them out to read them. So right from the beginning of school the children learnt how to blend sounds to make words and they could start to read sentences with those words straight away. The report noted that while all of the children in the study learnt to read, the children who learnt via Synthetic Phonics were 7 months ahead in both reading and spelling following the training period. The latter method was a far more efficient method to teach literacy. The researchers went on to say that Synthetic Phonics, taught first and fast, was the most effective way to teach literacy in the beginning stages. This was a very different way of teaching phonics from the way our grandparents were taught.

Current Thoughts

There has been ongoing debate worldwide about the relative benefits of using a Phonic or Whole Language approach to teach reading. Most western governments have conducted large scale reviews of the research over the last twenty years and have proclaimed that reading tuition must include Phonic instruction. The Whole Language approach has evolved into what is called the *Balanced Approach* and does include some phonic instruction, however, it does not use the Synthetic Phonic approach of first and fast, in a structured sequential way.

In Australia today, teachers and schools need to demonstrate that they are teaching the Phonic system in a structured sequential way, and Universities have to ensure that they instruct pre-service teachers in such a method. The University of Adelaide recently launched a free online course for teachers so that they can catch up on the Synthetic Phonics approach if they did not learn about it during their degree.

Why am I telling parents of young children about this? It is so that you will understand the importance of letters and sounds in learning to read and the steps you can take to ensure your child is well prepared for what is to come at pre-school and school. **I am not suggesting, however, that it is a parent's job to try to teach phonics.** Leave that to the teachers as they have been trained how to do it correctly. As a parent, you can focus on nursery rhymes and language games while helping your child to recognise and copy their name. These are the building blocks a teacher can work with to turn your child into a reader and writer.

I would like to mention one more group of studies that give us insights into early language and literacy development. New Zealand researcher Bill Tunmer, along with Andrew Nesdale investigated children's ability to segment the sounds of words they hear and how that was related to reading (Journal of Educational Psychology, 1985). The findings of that study and their following studies demonstrated that one of main things children needed to have before they can learn to read, is a good grasp of the sound system of the English language, this is known as *Phonemic Awareness*.

Sounds in English

Although there are 26 letters of the Alphabet, the letters go together in various ways to make 44 sounds. For example, the word *cat* is made up of three sounds *c-a-t*. Examples of letters that go together to make new sounds are; *sh* in *ship; ar* in *star* and *oy* in *boy*. Children learn to read more quickly when they can identify and manipulate the **sounds** they hear in **spoken** words before they learn to match sounds to letters to make and break words. A 2006 study by Tunmer, Chapman, and Prochnow, (in the *New Zealand Journal of Educational Studies*) found that children's knowledge of letter names, phonemic awareness and vocabulary at the beginning of school had an impact on their reading comprehension in Year 7. Then a study by Tunmer and Prochnow in 2009 (in *The Politics of Conformity in New Zealand*: Pearson), found that without direct instructional support, phonemic awareness eludes up to 25% of middleclass children in Year 1, and a lot more children from backgrounds that focus less on literacy. These studies demonstrated what children need to know before they can learn to read and how some children can slip behind if they don't get it. Similar studies in more recent years have confirmed that the development of those pre-literate factors have a significant impact on children's reading when they start school and as they progress through the school years.

I discuss beginning literacy in more detail in the next book for parents of children already in school. It is in the planning stages at the moment, but look out for it in 2026.

Other factors

Now let's get back to other reasons why learning to read does not come naturally. One reason has to do with book language. For example, the language used in books is usually different from the language we use when speaking. Open any fairy story – you know how it begins: 'Once upon a time…..' A phrase we never use in everyday speech.

Alphabet, number books and non-fiction books have different formats to regular story books too. Then there are children's books written as rhymes. In addition, numerous famous people have published 'children's books' but these are of variable quality. Later on, I will give you some tips on choosing good quality children's books to read to and with your child. At the moment, I want to concentrate on language and what you as a parent can do.

The path is through oral language, and you are probably already doing a number of things that will help your child to develop good language and pre-literacy skills. In fact, you can do this, no matter how young they are, or when you begin. Even a baby in a crib can hear you sing a lullaby or chant a nursery rhyme. If your child is already at school, many of the activities and games will still be beneficial. For parents of school aged children, look out for the next book in this series, which will be about how parents can support their children as they are learning to read and write at school.

In the following chapters we will discover lots of ways you can nurture your child's language and pre-literacy development. These include:

- How to create a stimulating environment
- How to create a language-rich environment,
- How to be a language model
- How to be a language model if you speak another language at home.
- How to expand a child's vocabulary
- How to make the most of everyday conversations
- Singing songs and reciting rhymes
- Language games
- Reading aloud
- Writing and typing
- Using technology
- Checklist for Kindergarten
- Checklist for school

One thing you can do straight away is to read to your child. You may already be doing this, if so, great, keep going. Regular reading together is a good start. If it is not something that happens in your household, begin this evening, after dinner, at your child's bedtime. Let them choose the book and look on together as you read. If you are not comfortable reading aloud, instead, ask them about the pictures and get them to make up a story about it. This helps to develop their spoken language skills as well as drawing on their imagination. In the next two chapters we will look at lots of ways to enrich your child's world and their oral language experiences.

Read to your child every day

CHAPTER 2

HOW CAN I MAKE MY CHILD'S WORLD RICHER AND MAKE IT FUN?

In this chapter we are talking about the home environment your child is born into. The early years of a child's life lays the foundation for their future growth and development. Children flourish when they live in a warm, safe environment with plenty of things to do and play with and surrounded by parents, grandparents or carers who give them the gift of their time and attention.

As parents, you play a crucial role in supporting your child's early learning and preparing them for preschool. By fostering a nurturing environment and engaging in meaningful interactions, you can enhance their cognitive, social, and emotional skills. One of the ways to do that is to make sure your child has a stimulating environment.

Back in the 1980s, Shirley Brice Heath wondered about the impact of the culture and environment in which children grew up, on how they fared at school. She spent a number of years observing the children and families in two small towns in America. In one town most of the parents worked at the local mill. Their hours were long, but they valued family and community connections and socialising together. They did not have books or educational toys in their homes, and reading to children was not considered very important. The reading that took place in their homes was in connection to bills, shopping lists or notices, and was done by the adults. In the other town the parents placed more emphasis on reading for enjoyment and on education. They frequently read to their children and had educational toys in their homes.

Heath's ethnographic study *Ways with Words* (Cambridge University Press, 1983) found that the children who grew up in an environment in which reading and learning were valued made more progress in the beginning years of school. She followed up that study with another when the children were in Gade 7 and found that the children who were more advanced in the first study were still well ahead of the children whose parents who did not place as much importance on reading, learning and education.

How do we as parents ensure that our home has 'a stimulating environment'?

1. **Creating a Rich, Stimulating Environment:**

   You can create a stimulating environment at home by providing a range of different toys, books, and games that are just right for you child's age. As children grow so quickly and sometimes lose interest in a toy that was once a favourite, find out if there is a toy library in your area. Once you join it is usually free to borrow toys and games, and you can change them as often as you like.

   If you have a pin up board in your home you could pin up some postcards or pictures of people from other cultures or views from different countries. Your child could help you find pictures from old magazines. These pictures can be used for conversations.

Encourage exploration, curiosity, and creativity through activities that promote sensory and motor development. Simple things like building blocks, puzzles, drawing and musical instruments are a good place to start. These enhance problem-solving skills, hand-eye coordination, and imagination

Incorporate sensory-rich activities with toys, music, and art projects.

For example:

- *Building castle or forts with blocks. If you don't have blocks, save up empty containers, such as tissues boxes and plastic containers.*

- *Jigsaw puzzles help with seeing shapes, hand eye coordination and manipulative skills*

- *Playing with musical instruments like drums or maracas. Maracas can be made by placing some large raw beans or peas or other items inside a cardboard roll from the kitchen and covering it with pretty paper and gluing it closed so that the beans can't spill out.*

- *If you can bear it, you could give them some pots and pans and a wooden spoon.*

- *Painting on big sheets of paper with big brushes. If that is too messy for your place, let them paint with water on outside walls or the deck.*

CHAPTER 2: HOW CAN I MAKE MY CHILD'S WORLD RICHER AND MAKE IT FUN?

What would you do to make the room more stimulating?

- *Neighbourhood walk. A walk down your street or to the local shops lets your child observe different houses, or shops they could tell you what they see or what they like.*

- *Role playing. If you are doing the prior suggestions already, have you tried role-playing games involving toys. For example, if they are playing with a toy car, you could suggest that they pretend there is a problem with the motor and that you are the garage owner. Then you have a conversation around that. You can put on a funny voice to make it more fun. Or if your child is playing with a doll you can suggest that the doll wants to go shopping and you could set up a pretend shop with small items to 'buy'.*

- *Let your imagination run wild with other scenarios. If you don't want to be part of a role play, perhaps suggest that a teddy is the garage owner or a different doll is the shopkeeper and the child can play both parts using different voices.*

2. Encouraging Independent Skills:

Developing independence is crucial for a child's self-confidence and readiness for preschool. Doing things for themselves will instil a sense of self, responsibility and promote motor skills.

Encourage your child to practice self-help skills such as

- Feeding themselves
- Dressing
- Using the toilet independently

    Use encouraging language and affirming their ability by saying things such as: Good job, you ate all of your dinner by yourself; You went to the toilet just like a big person, well done; What a clever cat you are, putting on your rain coat by yourself.

- Tidying up toys. This is a big one. It is often difficult to get children to pack away their toys after they have played with them. After accidentally stepping on Lego pieces too many times, I used a small, colourful baby sheet for Lego. It was then much easier to contain all of the pieces while they played, and fun for the children to help gather up the corners of the sheet and tip them into the Lego box.

    Another trick for picking up toys, is to count together as each toy is picked up. Perhaps have a competition to see who can pick up the most. This reinforces counting skills and makes a tedious chore more fun.

- Organizing their belongings. Start with small things that can be fun. Let them help to organise where toys go in their bedroom.

- It can be fun for a child to pack a small lunchbox with a snack and a drink, before a walk to the park.

- Promote Social Interaction:

  Social skills are vital for a child's success in school and beyond. Arranging playdates, at your house or at the park, with one friend to begin with.

- Provide opportunities for your child to interact with peers, siblings, and other family members, such as visiting Nana, getting big brother or sister play a game with them.

- Engage in group activities. Check out whether there is a parent and child group in your neighbourhood. There may be reading sessions for pre-schoolers at the local library. This helps them learn to share, take turns, and cooperate.

- Modelling positive social behaviour and empathy at home also helps them understand emotions and develop strong interpersonal skills.

- Saying something like; 'I understand you are upset that Billy would not share the truck with you. I know he is going through a hard time at the moment, so do you think maybe we can forgive him this time.' OR 'I understand how you feel, it can be hard for some children to share. What can we do so that you and Billy can be better friends?'

3. **Establishing a Routine:**

   A predictable routine helps children feel secure and fosters a sense of structure. Establish:

   - consistent meal times,
   - playtime, and
   - rest periods to create a balanced daily routine. This not only aids in establishing healthy habits but also promotes time management skills and self-regulation, which are essential for a successful transition to preschool.
   - Bed time. Children feel safe and secure when they know that their lives follow a regular pattern, and part of this is an established bedtime. It can be fun for them to put a favourite doll or teddy to bed, prior to their own bedtime.

4. **Encouraging a Love for Learning:**

   Parents can cultivate a love for learning by embracing their child's natural curiosity and fostering a positive attitude towards learning

   - Encourage their interests whether it be in books, toys, cooking
   - Support their exploration of various subjects.
   - Provide age-appropriate books, puzzles, and educational apps that align with their interests.

- Engage in activities that involve counting, sorting, matching, and problem-solving.

- Ask for their help with certain tasks, such as stirring a cake mixture, setting the table, putting away groceries.

5. **Emphasising Emotional Well-being:**

Developing emotional intelligence is crucial for a child's overall well-being and academic success.

- Help your child recognize and express their emotions by labelling feelings and providing a safe space for open communication. We have all heard the phrase 'use your words' it is a good standby when children are upset and emotional to help them express their feelings. You sometimes can help by stating 'I can see that you are angry'

- Teach them simple coping strategies like taking deep breaths or engaging in calming activities when they experience challenging emotions.

- Nurture a supportive and loving home environment that fosters their emotional growth.

This chapter focussed on how to build a warm, safe and enriching environment for your child. The following chapter covers how to build a language rich environment.

CHAPTER 3

HOW CAN I CREATE A LANGUAGE RICH WORLD?

What is a language rich world, and how do we create it? You might be thinking 'We talk a lot in our household. The TV or radio is on. I chat with friends and family, so my child can hear talk, off and on, all day long. Isn't this a language rich environment?' It is a start, but you can make it more rewarding and effective at increasing your child's understanding of how language works and increase their vocabulary.

First of all, I will talk about why it's important to develop the vocabulary and language skills of children before they get to school. There is a huge difference in the number of words that different children know when they go to school. Some children might only know a few thousand words, while other children may have a bank of tens of thousands of words. You will find that the children with vast word banks, have had lots of books read to them, are often talkative children who are interested in words, use interesting words and are always trying to find out the meaning of words. Those children understand far more words than others, before they get to school. When the teacher starts to teach the class to read, it is easy to predict which children will be able to read and understand more words than other children, who have not developed a wide vocabulary.

CHAPTER 3: HOW CAN I CREATE A LANGUAGE RICH WORLD?

Language development plays a crucial role in a child's overall growth and success in school. As a parent, you have a unique opportunity to foster your preschool child's language skills and lay a strong foundation for their future communication abilities and success at learning read. Following are a few examples of how you can increase the quantity and quality of your child's language experiences at home.

Increasing Your Child's Language Experiences

You could provide engaging things to look at and talk about, such as posters, cards and colourful books. For Example: Hanging a poster of children in another country on the wall, or putting up a picture that has some words on it. Have a special place in your child's room for picture books and prop one up so that the cover and title can be seen. This book could be changed regularly, so that even if you don't have time to read to them every day, they will see books and titles constantly.

In the meantime, find little bits of time throughout the day to focus on talking with your child. Make sure you are not asking constant questions, such as, 'What are you going to do at your friend's house?' or 'What did you do at kindy today?' Those questions often do not work at all - you will get a shrug, or the answer 'Not much'.

Engaging in meaningful conversations with your child is an excellent way to enhance their language development. Listen attentively to their thoughts and ideas, responding with interest and expanding on their statements. Ask open-ended questions that require more than a simple 'yes' or 'no' response, encouraging them to express their thoughts and opinions.

- Talk about objects and actions in your child's environment, using descriptive words.
- Encourage them to describe their experiences and feelings.

- Additionally, engage in activities like word games, naming objects, and discussing their attributes to expand their vocabulary.

Look at their interests and engage them and chat about something that they're interested in. Alternatively, if you notice something that you think they will find interesting introduce it and talk about it. I like to think about finding the 'teachable moments' in a day.

Conversations

For example, on the way home from the shops or Kindy you notice dark clouds overhead, you might say:

'Wow, look at those dark clouds. I wonder if it might rain'.

Or perhaps you notice a boy walking a dog. You could say: *'I wonder what that doggie is going to eat for dinner?'*

If the child does not respond you might make a silly suggestion such as: *'I wonder if it is ice-cream and custard.'* Your child is sure to point out that that dogs don't eat that. Or you might say *' Do you think it will eat beef, chicken, fish or dog biscuits?'*

Even asking *'What do you think?'* should get them thinking and elicit a reply.

Either scenario could lead to a discussion, such as which clouds produce rain, or when it rains (summer or winter), or what animals eat, what humans eat, what is good to eat. Each of these discussions would develop a child's knowledge about the world around them as well as developing vocabulary and greater understanding of language. Some of these ideas will be expanded in future chapters.

Learning language isn't just about learning lots of different vocabulary though, learning the words and what they mean, it's also about learning about the language structure too.

A Few Words About Grammar

In English, our language structure is different from most other languages. The structure of language is about word order. In English we have, broadly speaking, two types of words. They are words that are about the content of sentences (Content words) and we've got other helper words (Function words).

The Content words are *nouns*, such as the names of people, places and things. Other Content words are: *verbs*, that tell what is happening; *adjectives*, words that describe nouns, and *adverbs* that describe verbs. For example: In the phrase *the big red bus,* the word *bus* is a noun and the words *big red* are adjectives. If we add to the phrase and write the sentence *The big red bus went fast*. The word *went* is a verb and the word *fast* is an adverb.

The word *the* is a Function word. Other Function words are: *and, in, on, around, between, beside*, and many more.

Together the Content and Function words are necessary for us to make meaning and understand the overall message. The Content words really give us most of the meaning of a sentence, but the Function words are also necessary to fine tune the meaning. It is harder for children to learn the meaning of Function words, than Content words. That is why teachers in the early years place an emphasis on ensuring that children understand prepositions, a particular type of Function word that tells us position. For example, very young children often mix up *in* and *on*, which can be quite important in understanding a sentence in a story. Is the character *in the car* or *on the car?*

In English we have a particular structure in the way we put words together. We say *The big red bus goes fast,* but in another language, those words may be in a different order. Children are not just learning the words, they are learning the way that words have to go together in English. Did you learn another language at school? If so, you will be aware of the different structure of that language. For example: In French often the adjectives go in a different place to where they go in English. In English we say, *'The girl has blond hair'*, but in French it is, *'The girl has hair blond'*. When we use full sentences, we are helping children to understand the structure of English.

Further, in English, question forms are different to the way questions are structured in many other languages. When we ask questions, we might say *'How fast did the big red bus go?"* You may notice that the verb changed to a different form and got split in two (from *went* to *did go*).

We could also ask *'Did the big red bus go fast?'* Once again the verb has changed its form and been split up. You don't need to worry about this, just be aware that it is easier for your child to understand our complex language when you use whole sentences and questions. You are helping your child begin to understand that structure. This is important when they start to read books, because they'll see sentences and questions written down. There is more detail about language structure and how children learn it in Chapter 4.

The Differences Between Children

Some children are really chatty when they are little. They talk about everything all the time, while other children don't seem to talk much at all. They take everything in and they may be very active but don't talk a great deal. I noticed this difference between my own children. One of my sons was very active when he was little. He used to love being out in the back yard on his tricycle, riding round and round and making all sorts of *brm brm* noises. He wasn't too bothered about speaking. He would come inside to ask for things if he was hungry or thirsty, but most of the time he was happy playing on his own with cars, bikes, playing in the dirt or building things.

In contrast, my daughter seemed to want to be around me all the time and was constantly talking and chatting. I must admit, I got so sick of the '*Why*' question. For example: *Why do elephants have wrinkles?, Why is the lion asleep? Why do monkeys have long tails? Why does it smell funny? Why do we have to go home?* (You can tell we were at the zoo!)

You have probably experienced these differences between the talk each child uses too. Even within the same family, there can be huge differences between the amount that each child talks. It does tend to be girls who develop language faster and easier than boys do. Boys certainly catch up, but often when some boys are little, they may not speak as much as girls do.

How can we encourage the language of those children who don't speak as much as their peers or siblings? What we are looking for is for them to develop an understanding of the language even if they don't produce much. One way is to take advantage of bedtime. As you tuck them in, talk to them about what's coming up tomorrow, or what's planned for the next few days. These sorts of conversations with young children help to build their concept of time, along with an understanding of language.

Talking and Listening

There are two types of language that we all use. The first is *expressive language*. That can be related to what we say when we talk, in other words when we are expressing ourselves. The other form of language is *receptive language.* Receptive language is an understanding of the vocabulary and language that we hear, even if we don't use those words ourselves.

If you can think back to when you learnt another language at school, or when you visited another country, you can usually understand a lot more words and sentences than you can say. This is the difference between *expressive* and *receptive* language. If we go back to thinking about the child who does not talk much, it is important to expose them to lots of language, so that they have heard words and sentences in lots of situations and different contexts, so they can develop an understanding of what those words mean, even though they don't yet say them.

We want to develop both *expressive* and *receptive* language in all of our children. I have talked about just having conversations with your children, or talking with them about what they're doing, or what they're going to do. Another way is to look at their interests. I will use my son, who loved riding bikes and was interested in cars, as an example.

Can Books Help to Develop Language?

When we went to the library, I found a book all about cars and other things that moved. When we looked at the book together, we could talk about what makes a car go fast, or which goes faster, a plane or a motorbike, or which goes slower. In this way, we are starting to develop more language by using a book as a reference. I did not read this book as it was written for older children and would be boring and difficult for my son at his young age. I also found some pictures of cars in magazines that I cut out and stuck on a larger piece of paper to make a home-made poster.

Most children go through a stage, usually around four or five years of age, when they are interested in dinosaurs. A book about dinosaurs or a dinosaur poster is a terrific way to develop help you to develop your child's language. A lot of young children surprise you in that they know all the dinosaur names and can identify a number of them, from Tyrannosaurus Rex to the Brontosaurus and the Pterosaurs.

With a book or poster you can talk about which dinosaur is the biggest, which is the smallest, or which is the fiercest. In this way you are not only developing your child's vocabulary, you are developing an understanding of different concepts, such as big and small, fast and slow, and the ways to describe them. Children need to learn and understand these concepts at school for comparison and contrast activities, that aim to consolidate the ideas behind the concepts.

No matter how much expressive language your child currently uses, or what age they are right now, you can start to increase the amount and quality of language they are exposed to at home. The more you help develop their language now, the more prepared they will be for literacy lessons at school.

In the next chapter we will look at how children learn language and what happens if they hear more than one language at home.

CHAPTER 4

HOW DO WE LEARN TO SPEAK?

Children are born into a world of sound. From the earliest age, babies can recognise their mothers' voices. Even before they understand any words, they tend to get upset when someone uses an angry tone, and are soothed by a calm, gentle voice. It is as if humans are pre-programmed to learn and understand language, for no matter which country or culture we are born into, we will speak the language of our parents, or carers. Some lucky children grow up to be bi-lingual. No matter which language group a child lives in, the general environment in the home is very important for their language development.

In the last chapter we looked at how to make your child's world '*language rich*', but now I would like to go back even further and think about how we learnt to talk. I would like you to take just a moment to think about what you can remember about learning to talk. Think of the languages you heard at birth, if you heard more than one language. Recall an interaction around language that you experienced.

When I tried this activity, I remembered my mother singing me to sleep as a very early memory. I can also remember being told to go outside and play, I was often by myself and it was very boring, so I remember trying to make up games to play while I was outside. I do remember sneaking in and picking up the telephone and punching in numbers and trying to find somebody to talk to. I got into trouble for that one. I can also remember my grandfather telling me fairy stories.

So, think about your own memories of learning language and which activities helped you to learn more language. Now think about your child's first words. What were your child's first words? They are often Mum and Dad but following that, words are often the names of favourite toys, or they might mention a brother or sister's name. Quite often the words or names are not pronounced correctly, and later on, it becomes a family joke. Never try to correct a very young child's first attempts to say a new word or name. Just make sure that you use it correctly when speaking to the child.

Some of the questions we will look at in this chapter are

- Why is language development so important?
- What areas of the brain are used for language?
- How do children learn language?
- What are the stages of language learning?
- Do parents teach children to speak?
- Why learn about language acquisition?

Why is language development so important?

Language is what separates us from other animals. Now I know what you're going to tell me that your dog understands a lot of the instructions or the commands that you give him, and parrots can talk, and I know that a number of monkeys have been trained to understand a lot of human speech, however those understandings are at much lower level than what humans are able to comprehend. Some animals might understand a few things we say and might be able to act on them, but they can't then generate the same language to talk with you or think about more complex ideas, so I'll stand by my original statement that it separates us from other animals.

Also language is really important for the socialisation of human beings. That means because we have language we are able to connect with other human beings we may not know, or who are not in our family. We can learn more about them, about their values or about what they think, by using language.

We also learn about the world around us through language. Human knowledge can be passed on from one generation to the next through language. Initially everything was through oral language. The elders of a tribe would pass on their knowledge to the next generation verbally, sometimes in song, so that the culture grew with the common language.

Since we developed writing we have been able to put our thoughts and ideas into books, so it can be passed on that way. This also means that we don't always have to have first-hand experience to learn and understand others or facts about the world. We can look up what we want to know or find out in a book or the internet. These days most people will look on YouTube to find out how to do things, and those items are visual and verbal. I believe that language is also a key part of that, whether it's reading and writing or whether it's listening to somebody else. It is accumulated knowledge that is able to be passed on through language. Culture is also passed on through language. When researchers looked at different ancient tribes, they found that some tribes had different ways of analysing colours. For example in Eskimo languages there are many descriptions or descriptive words for the different colours and types of snow. We might recognise snow as white, perhaps recognising a bluish or greyish tinge.

Some African tribes name a whole range of colours within the ochre, yellow and brown range that other cultures do not recognise. We may see those shades but would not usually try to differentiate them in everyday language. Those African tribes however, analysed and differentiated those shades of colours differently, as they were important for them. They do that differentiation through their language, so that there is a shared cultural understanding of those colours. Using colours is a very simple example of how culture is passed on through language. All other parts of culture and society norms are introduced through language.

Our understanding of what it means to be an Australian, or an American, or an Aboriginal person is passed on mostly through language. Further, language and linguistic symbols give us powerful tools for thought. Our thoughts are through language and that means that we are able to think about really complex ideas because we are using language in our minds to think about things. What we are doing now, thinking about language and how it works, is called *Metalinguistic Awareness.* Children begin to develop this awareness when they start to learn about the sound system of language and how it works.

What areas of the brain are used for language?

The parts of the brain involved in language began to be recognised in 1861 when Paul Brocca, a French neurosurgeon, examined the brain of recently deceased man called Tan. When he was alive, Tan couldn't speak, and could only say the word 'Tan', however he could understand speech. Brocca found Tan had no impairment in his mouth or his tongue but when his brain was dissected following his death, he found a large lesion in the area that's now called Broca's area, which is in the left frontal cortex, the area for speech. Ten years later, Wernicke, a German neurologist, discovered the part of the brain involved in understanding language, which is in the posterior left temporal lobe. Another part of the brain involved in language is a neural loop, involved in both understanding and producing language. The Broca and Wernicke areas are connected by a large bundle of nerve fibres, see the drawing below.

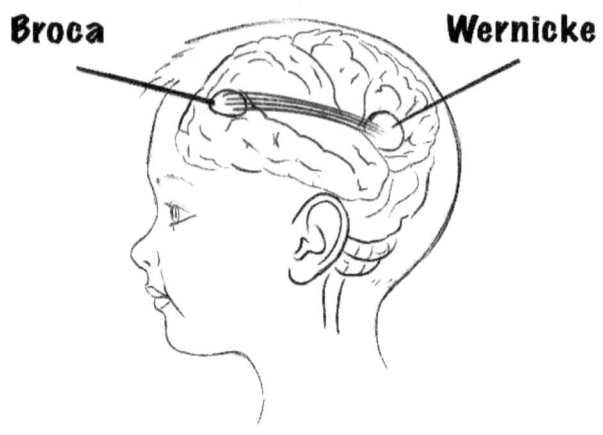

Where Language sits in the brain.

Areas of the brain used for understanding the grammar of a language are more vulnerable to altered language input, for example, when a person is deaf or they hear poor speech from others.

The contribution of the right hemisphere to language is in understanding Denotations, (dictionary definitions of a word) and Connotations (the meaning of a word in a local context). Further, the message depends not just on what is said but how it is said. When a person has damage to the right side of the brain they can't comprehend metaphors. For example, if they are asked to point to the picture which depicts '*He is a night owl*', and are shown one picture of a boy sitting at a desk studying under a small lamp and another picture of an owl in a tree at night-time, they will choose the owl.

How do children learn language?

No matter which language your child is born into he or she will learn it. Babies as young as three days old find adult speech rewarding. Psychologists did some experiments with very young children and found that even babies one month old would react to changes in adult speech. A child must perceive the sounds and then produce the sounds in order to understand and be understood. This means that first of all the child needs to distinguish speech sounds from other sounds we humans make such as sneezing, coughing, laughing, humming, sighing, throat clearing, grunting and clicking.

It doesn't matter which language group any child is born into, by the age of eight months they're already in tune with the language, the way it sounds and they start to filter out other things. If you are a little child born in Africa, in the cultural and language group that has clicks as part of their speech, by 8 months you would recognise that as part of speech. However, if you were born to an English speaking parent, (and we don't have clicks as part of our language), then after eight months, if you heard somebody making clicking sounds, you wouldn't recognise that as something that belonged in speech

Children learn the language they hear from birth.

It seems crazy that by 8 months old we are filtering out the sounds of speech or intonations that aren't in our language. I will use a tonal language as another example. In tonal languages intonation patterns vary within words. In Mandarin the word 'Ma' has many different meanings including mother and horse, depending on whether it is said with a high tone or a low tone, and whether the tone is rising or falling. In English we tend to use intonation patterns for phrases rather individual words. For example, in the sentence, 'I am going to the shops in the morning.' there are 3 phrases:

>I am going

>to the shops

>in the morning

Try saying them. What do you notice about the way your voice rises and falls? We tend to use the same level for all of the words in the phrase, except for the third phrase. In that one, our voice goes down at the end to indicate the end of the sentence.

Young babies learn the sounds of their parents' language but they also learn to associate meanings with those sounds. Languages are complicated, but even little babies seem to be able to learn to speak and understand them. An American Linguist and theorist, Naom Chomsky who has studied how we learn to speak over many decades, said that humans act as if we have an inbuilt 'Language Acquisition Device' (LAD). LAD does not physically exist, but as babies, we act as though it does. He discusses his theories in the book *On the Nature, Acquisition and Use of Language,* which can be found online.

What are the stages of language learning?

Most children go through the same stages of learning a language so in the beginning, when they're really little babies, from when they born to about 8 weeks it's mostly reflexive types of sounds including crying. From around 8 to 20 weeks they start to laugh and make cooing and gooing sounds. Between 16 and 30 weeks they start to play with sounds such as buh, buh and mum mum. From 25 to 50 weeks they babble saying dada, gaga, mum mum. Between 9 and 12 months little children start to use their first words. They still do some of the babbling, but it will be varied and overlap with their first words. Then between 12 and 18 months they're really starting to say quite a lot of single words. From 18 months and two years children begin to use two-word utterances such as *'dad car', 'mummy shoe', 'more bickie', 'want teddy'.* These two-word utterances are called 'telegraphic speech,' as the child uses them to convey a wider meaning just like a telegram. From 2 to 3years, children use three and four word sentences and at 4 to 5 years have a greater understanding of the language they hear and can use increasingly complex grammar.

So what do the children have to learn? As well as the 44 sounds that make up English words, they need to learn the meaning of those words and how the words go together to make up sentences. Then they need to interpret what those sentences mean according to the context.

Do parents teach children to speak?

When researchers first started looking at how children learn to speak, they believed that children just imitated what their parents did and copied them. Certainly, there is a percentage of imitation, but most of the time we, as adults, don't speak in full sentences, particularly to children. Researchers found that parents use a modified form of language when speaking to very young children, they call it 'Motherese'. It is a very simplified form of language that we think young children will understand better than the way we speak to adults. Some researchers started to record parents who were trying to teach their children to use correct grammatical structure. For example a child might say 'I wants bickie' and the parent might say: 'You mean, I want a bickie' and the child repeats, 'Yes I wants bickie'. Then the parent emphasises 'I **want a** bickie'. The child does not pick up on the different correct form, but focusses on the meaning. Researchers found that children won't understand grammatical structures until they are ready to do so.

Back in 1973, Brown published a book titled *A First Language* (Harvard University Press) that was about how we learn the grammar of English. He had noted down when his son began to use particular parts of language. He and other researchers then investigated the early language structures of other children and found that they acquired English grammar in much the same order. Following is the order most children learn the first 8 of 14 aspects of English grammar as discovered by Brown.

ITEM	EXAMPLE
1. -ing	Play**ing**
2. in	**in** the house
3. on	**on** the bed
4. plural -s	cat**s**, book**s**
5. past tense (irregular)	ate, ran
6. possessive -s	Bill**'s** car
7. is, are	Guess where he **is**
8. past tense (regular)	walk**ed**, jump**ed**

CHAPTER 4: HOW DO WE LEARN TO SPEAK?

Don't worry if your child seems to learn the grammar in a slightly different order. I have given you the information that Brown discovered simply as a guide, so that you will not worry if your child has not yet worked out some aspects of English.

English speaking children produce and learn the grammar through a process that includes some imitation, but it mostly includes trying to work things out for themselves. Often, they will have worked something out and use it correctly for a while, then apply it incorrectly. For example, children learn irregular past tenses such as the past tense of 'go' as 'went'. Then they learn to talk about the past by using words like 'walked', 'chopped' and 'coughed'. They worked out that by adding *ed* to a word, we can talk about things that have already happened. Then they over apply that rule and say things like: '*We goed to the shops*' or '*we wented to the shops*'. Children go through a phase when you think they've learned the correct structure, and then all of a sudden they over apply it, and don't seem to remember the correct version. It takes them quite a while to work out how to use and understand the grammar of any language. A few other examples of English that make learning the language difficult are:

We say	**But we don't say**
I went to school	*I went to movie*
We went to the river	*We went to **the** Lake Ayre*
A ball hit him on the arm	*A ball hit him on **an** arm*

It takes time for children to work out how to use the correct structure. Questions and passive forms take even longer to understand. For example, If shown a picture of a girl wearing a blindfold and asked '*Is it easy to see the girl?*' young children would say '*No*' because the girl can't see. They focus on the meaning which is the most import thing for them. Learning the structure takes practise and they do some copying but they can't pick it up until they're ready to do so. Parents correcting them doesn't usually work until they are ready. This was partly where that idea of the 'language acquisition device' came from. The idea that we seem to have an inbuilt capacity to work out language as we grow. Other theorists think that the influence of language in a social situation is also important. They feel that we should think about language being acquired through all of our social interactions.

Why learn about language acquisition?

We often underestimate what young children are able to understand as they can usually understand a lot more language than what they can produce and understanding a little bit about how language is acquired will help you as a parent to perhaps do more with your language and expose your child at a younger age to more language, so that they will learn and develop their language more quickly which will then help them later on as they start to get into Kindy and school.

CHAPTER 5

How Can I be a Language Model?

As a parent, you are your child's first and most influential language teacher. From the moment they are born, your words, tone, and gestures shape their understanding of language and communication. By intentionally modelling rich and meaningful language, you lay the foundation for their future literacy, social skills, and academic success. Parents serve as powerful language models for their children. Use clear language when speaking to them, with correct pronunciation and grammar. Avoid baby talk or using overly simplistic language, as it can hinder their language development. Actively engage in conversations as previously mentioned and expose them to a variety of rich and diverse language experiences.

Why Language Modelling Matters

Children learn language by listening to, working out meanings, imitating some speech patterns and vocabulary of those around them. Parents serve as role models, demonstrating how language is used in various contexts. Using clear, articulate speech and varied vocabulary helps children understand the richness of language. Additionally, parents can model conversational skills such as taking turns, listening actively, and responding appropriately.

Research shows that the amount and style of language parents use when conversing with their children is one of the strongest predictors of children's early language development. Children benefit from exposure to adult speech that is varied and rich in information about objects and events in the environment.

Those little brains are constantly working away at understanding the language they were born into. Some researchers (Carey and Bartlett) were interested in how this happens and used an inventive experiment to test how children learn one new word (Papers and Reports on Child Language Development, 1978, Stanford University).

They worked with 20, three-year-old children in a one-one setting. First, they assessed which colours the children knew by asking them to point out or give items to them. For example, if there were two toy cars, a red one and a yellow one, the child might be asked to point to the red car. The child knew what toy cars were and the colour red, so was able to do those tasks easily.

In the experiment, there were also two trays, one was a red plastic tray that the child was familiar with. The child knew the colour red and could identify red things when asked to point them out. The other tray was an olive colour, made of chromium. The researcher gave the child a small item and said: *'Please put it on the chromium tray.'* Even though none of the children had ever heard the word 'chromium' before, they correctly worked out which tray to put the items on. It seemed that they were able to use a process of elimination to work out that the correct tray, was the one that was not red. When reassessed later, the researchers found that not all of the children retained the word *chromium*, however, the study demonstrated that it is possible for children learn new words in a fast-tracked way. It is easy to underestimate young children's ability to learn language.

Their little brains are able to work out information about new words when they hear them in meaningful contexts.

Practical Ways to Model Language

Here are some effective strategies to enhance your child's language development:

- **Use Complete Sentences and Correct Grammar**: Speak in full sentences, even when your child is just beginning to talk even if those sentences are simpler than if you were speaking with an adult. For example, say, 'I am going to the shop to buy some milk and bread,' instead of 'Going to the shops'

- **Expand on Your Child's Speech**: If your child says, 'Dog bark,' you might respond, 'Yes, the dog is barking loudly. Is it because it sees a cat.' This technique, known as modelling, helps children learn new vocabulary and sentence structures.

- **Engage in Back-and-Forth Conversations**: Encourage your child to express themselves by asking open-ended questions like, 'What did you like about the story?' or 'How did that make you feel?'

- **Use Expressive Gestures and Facial Expressions**: Non-verbal cues like smiling, nodding, and using hand gestures can reinforce the meaning of words and make communication more engaging.

Embracing Multilingualism at Home

If your family speaks more than one language, expose your child to both or all languages from an early age. Speaking different languages at home exposes them to diverse vocabulary, cultural understanding, and cognitive benefits. It is however a good idea to keep the languages separate. If one parent speaks English as the mother tongue and the other speaks Spanish, it is best if each parent speaks to the child in their own mother tongue. This way the child hears a good model of each language and not a mixture of the two languages. As not only words, but grammatical structures differ in different languages, it is very difficult for a child to work out the grammatical structure of each language if they don't hear a good and consistent version.

Introduce the separate languages through songs, books, and games. For Example: Singing *'Head, Shoulders, Knees, and Toes'* in Spanish.

- Connect with bilingual communities and cultural events. For Example: Attending a cultural festival.

- Practice basic phrases and greetings in your different languages. For Example: *Greeting others with 'Hola' or 'Good morning.'*

If your family speaks more than one language, exposing your child to multiple languages from an early age can offer numerous cognitive, social, and cultural benefits. Research indicates that early exposure to multiple languages enhances children's problem-solving abilities, critical thinking skills, and cultural awareness.

Here are some ways to support multilingual development:

- **Integrate Your Languages into Daily Activities**: Use songs, books, and games in different languages. For example, singing or reciting rhymes in your mother tongue during the day. Then at night the other parent reads a bedtime story in their mother tongue, explaining the words and meaning. Some children's books are written in two languages with each language taking up one side of each double page. This can be helpful, as once the child knows the story well in one language you can read it the other language, Their understanding of the words and story in one language will help them to transfer that understanding to the other language.

- **Connect with Bilingual Communities**: Attend cultural festivals, language classes, or community events that celebrate different languages and cultures.

- **Maintain Consistency**: Regularly use each language in specific contexts or with certain family members to help your child differentiate and learn both languages effectively.

What sort of a Language Model are you?

Being a language model is about more than just talking to your child; it's about engaging them in meaningful conversations, exposing them to rich vocabulary, and encouraging their curiosity about language. By doing so, you equip them with the communication skills they need to succeed in school and beyond.

Remember, every word you speak, every story you tell, and every conversation you share contributes to your child's language development journey.

CHAPTER 6

HOW CAN I ENRICH MY CHILD'S VOCABULARY?

This section explores more strategies and techniques you as a parent can employ to support and enhance your child's language development during the preschool years. Introduce your child to a wide range of different and unusual vocabulary words to enrich their language skills. First, we will look at some of the research into vocabulary development to gain clues about how we can help our own children.

Early studies found that differences in children's vocabulary depended on whether the family was financially comfortable or poor, the level of the mother's education, father's employment, and the intelligence level of the child. In a book titled *The Meaning Makers: Children Learning Language and Using Language to Learn,* Gordon Wells followed 32 British children from their first birthdays to the end of their elementary education (Heinemann Educational Books, 1986). He looked at the factors mentioned above, and other differences that occurred in the homes to determine whether other factors were involved in developing language.

All of the factors just mentioned have an impact on school learning. However, when they are statistically controlled, other important factors emerge. Wells noted that whether parents read to the child and the types of conversations they had with their child were very important factors.

In the US, Catherine Snow wanted to know what happened in the families from poorer backgrounds, those with a low socio-economic status. In her 1983 research report, *Language and Literacy: Relationships during the Preschool Years (Harvard Educational Review)*. Catherine examined the language that mothers used with their children and what happened when parents read to their children. She thought that the **number** of words a child learnt was not as important as the **variety** of words and the context for learning. She wanted to find out if different words were used during an activity or book reading, and whether it impacted on later school success.

Over the next decades Catherine Snow and her colleagues continued to investigate how children learnt new words, and what sort of words made a difference to their understanding of the world around them and the world at large.

In a 2017 report, *The Role of Vocabulary Versus Knowledge in Children's Language Learning: a Fifty-year Perspective*, (which you can find online), she noted that many research studies have found that children's scores on measures of vocabulary predict their reading success. She indicated that some findings found that by the age of three, there are already large differences between children's vocabularies, and this is well before most children enter early childhood settings.

In one of the studies, she found that children's vocabulary performance in kindergarten and later in 2nd grade related more to the mother's use of more sophisticated words than to the number of words overall. She also noted that explicit vocabulary instruction in preschool, is much less efficient than the natural vocabulary learning that results from **parents**

using low frequency, uncommon words, during rich discussions about interesting topics. This is good news for you as a parent, as it tells us that we do not have to try to cram as many words as possible into our interactions with our children. However, it will help our children immensely if we use uncommon words in conversations or discussions in meaning contexts.

How to Introduce More Uncommon Words

It has been found that children who have the most comprehensive vocabularies when they begin school, had often been read non-fiction books (books with lots of facts in them, rather than a story). When parents read non-fiction books to children, they discuss the content and meaning in the books. This leads to the use of lots of uncommon words that the children would not usually hear. Children who are exposed to those meaningful discussions about facts, go on to develop more advanced literacy skills by the end of the first year of school, than children who have not listened to non-fiction books with the accompanying discussions.

The non-fiction books are usually in an area of the child's interest, for example, dinosaurs or transport vehicles. If you look at non-fiction books for children, you will find that they usually have more words on each page and that they use unusual vocabulary. Think about the book on dinosaurs, not only will it contain the names of different types of dinosaurs, but it will also have words like the *paleolithic age*, the *ice age*, *climate*, amongst other words, we do not use in everyday speech.

Even a book on transport may have unusual words such as *tip truck, front end loader, aeroplane, yacht, tanker, road train,* and may talk about the relative speed of vehicles, using words like acceleration, knots, miles or kilometres per hour. As there will be many words and concepts a child is not familiar with, the parent takes time to explain and discuss the meanings of those words. All of this discussion around the contents of a non-fiction book not only increased those children's vocabularies but gave them an understanding of a greater variety of words.

Finding Good Non-Fiction Books

Let us say you are going to the library and looking for some books to read with your child. I found a couple of really fabulous books in my local library that are worth looking for if you have pre-schoolers or young school aged children. One book, by Meredith Rowan and Monika Forsberg is called *Little Word Whizz: An Interesting Word for Every Day of the Year* (Magic Cat, 2021). Each double page of this picture book focusses on a theme for two weeks. Along the bottom of the page is the word for each day. It is not necessary to follow the suggested word list or to do it as a daily exercise. I believe the book has potential benefits without following the prescribed pattern. The illustrations in this book are entertaining as they depict different animals doing crazy things, so even if you don't use any of the words in the weekly lists, the pictures offer opportunities for discussion.

I certainly wouldn't be following the proposed format with a pre-school child. Instead, I would follow the child's interest and find the page that incorporated those interests. Then I would point to the illustration of an animal, and make some comment about what it was doing. Then ponder, 'I wonder why the dog is doing that?' and look to the child for their contribution. If the any of the words of the week were appropriate to the discussion, I would use them. There is one rider, and that is, the book is American and it begins with seasons as they are in the USA. For example: the first week's words and theme are based on temperature, so the animals depicted are in the snow, riding chair lifts, skiing down-hill, while wearing colourful beanies and jackets. Some of the pictures are funny. There are all sorts of words dotted across the pages and many of them would be too hard for little ones. We do use words to talk about temperature so we could discuss how cold it would be in the snow and how the animals stay warm. One of the animals looks scared, and the word is nervous. That is an unusual word that would be good to use as you talk about how the animal on the ski lift is feeling. You could talk about how you would feel if you were going up on a ski lift, would you be nervous or excited? You could then talk about other times when you feel nervous (going to the doctor, starting school) or excited (a birthday party).

On another double page there is a party going on. There are words like entertain, inspire, celebrate and overjoyed. Probably all of those words could be introduced in your discussion of the illustrations. You might even point to a word and say; 'This says *celebrate*, do you remember when we celebrated Grandma and Grandpa's wedding anniversary? That would be a good way to contextualize the word for your child, to make it more meaningful and more likely to be remembered.

Another example is the double page on art. The illustrations show cats painting, and cats in a painting. Some of the words include masterpiece and antique. If your child enjoys painting, you would be able to relate the context to their own pictures, which of course are masterpieces you have stuck on the fridge. You would need to choose which other words are appropriate for your child at their stage of development and understanding of language.

Little Word Whizz is one book with interesting little pictures in it that I think you could talk about and maybe add one or two of the words that you think are about right for your child. It is probably a book that could be used over a long period of time using different words as the child develops

CHAPTER 6: HOW CAN I ENRICH YOUR CHILD'S VOCABULARY

If your child is interested in in science, a picture book titled *1000 words STEM* by Jules Pottle may be of interest (Penguin, Random House, 2021). *STEM* stands for Science, Technology, Engineering and Mathematics. The forward states that it builds science vocabulary and literacy skills, so is aimed at slightly older children, but it is well set out and would be a good way to choose a topic of interest to your child and discuss aspects of that using some of the uncommon words on the page.

For example, one sections focuses on sound. If your child loves making sounds, there is a picture of a drum, and has the words *tap* and *beat*; there is also a picture of a guitar with the words *strings* and *pluck*; there's a dog, *bark*; a train, *clickety clack*, and many more. This section of the book talks about all the different sounds, so depending on the child's level of development and level of language, you can add as much or as little as you like.

Another section is about machines. We talked a little earlier about children who might be interested in vehicles. On the pages about machines, there is a bus and motorbikes. Using non-fiction picture books are a good way to build vocabulary and understanding of the environment around us, but they are the type of books that you would use every now and again until your child is old enough to be able to understand most of the words and you can graduate to reading them the sentences rather than just discussing the pictures.

I have talked a lot about books as the basis for discussion, however, we don't always have to have a book. We can talk about what we're doing, especially if the child is involved in the activity. For example, if we are chopping vegetables to go into soup, you can talk about what you are doing instead of just doing it quietly. You could say 'Let's peel the carrots and chop them up to put them in the soup. Then ask them what they think might go well in the soup and you could talk about whether that would work and whether it is in a cupboard or the fridge. This way all of the language and any new words you introduce becomes meaningful and related to them. There needs to be a good **context** for the language that you are using so that it just seems natural and not too contrived

More Ideas for developing language in preschool children

If your child is already in pre-school and you have **not** read lots of non-fiction books to them, it is not a lost cause. Start today. There are many other ways to help boost your child's vocabulary and understanding of language. Certainly, the earlier you start the better, and it doesn't have to be structured at all, except for the reading together. It is a good idea to set a time for that every day if you can.

- Introduce new words in context during daily activities. *(Example: Using the word 'gigantic' when describing a large tree.)*

- Encourage storytelling and imaginative play. *(Example: Acting out a pirate adventure.)*

The take home message for you today is to start to find some non-fiction books to read to your child. Every child has things they are interested in and curious about: maybe it is dance or ballet, cooking, race cars, how things are built, nature, birds, insects, animals. What is your child interested in? How many books on that and related topics can you find? The bookstore may not have many for pre-school children, so check your local library.

In this chapter we have investigated how you can develop your child's vocabulary prior to school. In the next chapter we will look at the role of singing and rhyme in helping to develop your child's language.

CHAPTER 7

LET'S ALL SING!

A few years ago, I met a much older woman who found out that I taught teachers. She told me that she used to be a First Grade teacher and asked what the latest methods and research said about how to teach reading. I mentioned some of the groundbreaking studies that were presented earlier in this book. Then I said how important it was for young children to know the sound system and to learn the letter-sound relationships. She replied ' *Ah nothing has changed. I always thought that if children knew their Nursery Rhymes they would be able to learn to read!!*' She had intuitively understood the importance of learning rhymes to help children understand the sounds that they hear, as they start to learn to read. Apart from the benefit to later reading there are other reasons to learn rhymes.

The Benefits of Singing Songs and Reciting Rhymes

Singing and rhyming are joyful activities, It is fun to recite rhymes and to do the actions that often come with them. As we noted before, they are essential tools for developing early language and literacy skills. They lay the foundation for phonemic awareness—the ability to hear, recognize, and play with the sounds in spoken language—which is a crucial step towards reading.

FROM RHYME TO READING: HOW LANGUAGE PLAY BUILDS TO LITERACY

Why Music and Rhyme Matter

Singing songs and reciting nursery rhymes expose children to the musicality of language—its rhythm, rhyme, and patterns. These features help children recognize the sounds within words, remember phrases, and anticipate what comes next. All of this builds important pre-reading skills in a fun, natural way.

How to Make the Most of Songs and Rhymes

Use Repetitive and Rhythmic Patterns Rhythmic songs like 'Twinkle, Twinkle, Little Star' or 'Baa Baa Black Sheep' help children notice syllables and word patterns, building memory and phonemic awareness.

Add Actions and Gestures

Pair songs with hand movements or body actions to enhance engagement and understanding. Try clapping along to 'If You're Happy and You Know It' or making spider movements with your fingers during 'Itsy Bitsy Spider.' These physical actions help connect words to meaning and improve coordination.

Include Songs from Different Cultures

Expose your child to songs from around the world. This introduces new sounds and cultural experiences. For example, 'Frère Jacques' in French is a simple, beautiful melody that encourages curiosity about other languages.

Sing Daily and Be Playful

Incorporate songs into daily routines—like singing a tidy-up song, a good morning greeting, or a lullaby at bedtime. The repetition and consistency provide structure and emotional comfort.

Making up rhymes

It can be fun for a child to make up rhymes. Together you could make up some new verses for known nursery rhymes. For example: Instead of Mary had a little lamb, you might say –

> Mary had a little cat
> It's fur was black as ink
> Everywhere that Mary went
> The cat would start to slink.

Another invention might be a variation of Hickory Dickory Dock –

> Hickory Dickory Deet
> The dog ran up the street
> The clock struck two
> The cat ran too
> Hickory Dickory Deet

If you are making up variations on nursery rhymes together with your child, any word that rhymes is acceptable, even those they are not real words. Below are a number of popular nursery rhymes. How many do you know? How many does your child know? Which ones will you recite with your child today?

1. Baa Baa Black Sheep

Verses:

> Baa baa black sheep, have you any wool?
> Yes sir, yes sir, three bags full.
> One for the master, one for the dame,
> And one for the little boy who lives down the lane.

Actions:

- Pretend to pat a sheep.
- Hold up three fingers for 'three bags full.'
- Point to three imaginary people.

2. Twinkle, Twinkle, Little Star

Verses:

> Twinkle, twinkle, little star,
> How I wonder what you are.
> Up above the world so high,
> Like a diamond in the sky.

Actions:

- Open and close hands above head like twinkling stars.
- Point up and form a diamond shape with fingers.

3. Mary Had a Little Lamb

Verses:

> Mary had a little lamb,
> Its fleece was white as snow.
> And everywhere that Mary went,
> The lamb was sure to go.

Actions:

- Pretend to pet a lamb.
- Walk in place as if leading a lamb.

4. Five Little Ducks

Verses:

> Five little ducks went out one day,
>
> Over the hills and far away.
>
> Mother duck said, 'Quack, quack, quack, quack!'
>
> But only four little ducks came back.

Actions:

- Hold up five fingers and waddle hand like ducks.
- 'Quack' with hands like a duck's bill.

5. Humpty Dumpty

Verses:

> Humpty Dumpty sat on a wall,
>
> Humpty Dumpty had a great fall.
>
> All the king's horses and all the king's men
>
> Couldn't put Humpty together again.

Actions:

- Rock side to side like sitting on a wall.
- Gently fall or clap hands on 'had a great fall.'

6. Hickory Dickory Dock

Verses:

> Hickory dickory dock,
> The mouse ran up the clock.
> The clock struck one,
> The mouse ran down.

Actions:

- Wiggle fingers up like a mouse climbing.
- Make a loud 'ding' on 'struck one' and run fingers down.

7. Rock-a-bye Baby

Verses:

> Rock-a-bye baby, on the treetop,
> When the wind blows, the cradle will rock.
> When the bough breaks, the cradle will fall,
> And down will come baby, cradle and all.

Actions:

- Rock arms like a baby.
- Sway gently for wind, then slowly lower arms for fall.

8. Itsy Bitsy Spider

Verses:

> The itsy bitsy spider climbed up the water spout.
> Down came the rain and washed the spider out.
> Out came the sun and dried up all the rain,
> And the itsy bitsy spider climbed up again.

Actions:

- Use fingers to climb like a spider.
- Wiggle fingers like rain, circle arms for sun.

9. Here We Go Round the Mulberry Bush

Verses:

> Here we go round the mulberry bush,
> The mulberry bush, the mulberry bush.
> Here we go round the mulberry bush,
> So early in the morning.

Actions:

- March or dance in a circle.
- Mime washing, brushing, or other morning activities.

10. Frère Jacques

Verses:

> Frère Jacques, Frère Jacques,
> Dormez-vous? Dormez-vous?
> Sonnez les matines! Sonnez les matines!
> Ding, dang, dong. Ding, dang, dong.

Actions:

- Pretend to sleep.
- Ring imaginary bells for 'ding dang dong.'

11. This Little Piggy

Verses:

> This little piggy went to market,
> This little piggy stayed home.
> This little piggy had roast beef,
> This little piggy had none.
> This little piggy cried wee, wee, wee all the way home.

Actions:

- Wiggle each toe or finger as the rhyme progresses.
- Tickle on 'wee wee wee.'

12. Bingo

Verses:

>There was a farmer had a dog,
>And Bingo was his name-o.
>B-I-N-G-O,
>B-I-N-G-O,
>B-I-N-G-O,
>And Bingo was his name-o.

Actions:

- Clap hands for each missing letter as the song repeats.
- Pretend to pat a dog.

13. Row, Row, Row Your Boat

Verses:

>Row, row, row your boat,
>Gently down the stream.
>Merrily, merrily, merrily, merrily,
>Life is but a dream.

Actions:

- Sit facing each other and pretend to row.
- Smile and sway together

These rhymes are more than just fun—they are foundational learning experiences disguised as play. Through music and movement, your child is developing critical skills that will support them as readers, listeners, and communicators.

Encourage your child to sing loudly, move freely, and enjoy the magic of rhyme. The joy of shared songs will create cherished memories and a strong foundation for future learning. What other songs and rhymes can you share with your child? Maybe there is a rhyme your mother taught you as a child. Or is there a favourite rhyming song that you learnt when you were at school? Sharing those experiences will be fun for both of you.

CHAPTER 8

LET'S PLAY LANGUAGE GAMES

Children learn best when they are having fun—and language games are a perfect way to combine learning with laughter. These games are not just entertaining; they're powerful tools that build communication, vocabulary, listening, memory, and critical thinking skills. Best of all, they can be played almost anywhere—with no special equipment needed.

Why Language Games Matter

Language games:

- Encourage children to express themselves.
- Improve listening and comprehension skills.
- Introduce new vocabulary in a natural, playful context.
- Build confidence in speaking and storytelling.
- Help develop memory, sequencing, and problem-solving skills.

Whether you have five minutes in the car or a whole afternoon indoors, language games turn everyday moments into fun, teachable ones.

Simple and Effective Language Games

1. 'I Spy' (With a Twist!)

This classic guessing game teaches descriptive language, categorization, and observational skills.

How to Play:

Say, *'I spy with my little eye, something that is red.'* Encourage your child to ask questions or guess the object.

Expand the Game:

- Use different categories: size, shape, function, or location (*'I spy something you can wear'*).

- Add letters: *'I spy something that starts with the letter B.'*

2. 'Simon Says'

This fun movement game supports listening, attention, and the ability to follow multi-step directions.

How to Play:

Give commands starting with 'Simon says' (e.g., *'Simon says touch your toes'*). If you don't say 'Simon says,' and they still do it—they're out!

Boost the Challenge:

- Use sequencing: *'Simon says touch your head, then hop twice.'*

- Add prepositions: *'Simon says put your hands **under** the table.'*

3. Story Starters & Role-Play

Storytelling builds narrative skills, creativity, and expressive language.

How to Play:

Begin with a prompt like, *'One day, a bear found a magic box...'* and take turns continuing the story.

Role-Playing Variation:

Dress up or use stuffed animals to act out scenes from favourite books or make up new adventures. Ask open-ended questions like, *'What do you think will happen next?'*

4. Word Play and Board Games

Games like **Scrabble Junior**, **Boggle**, or even simple rhyming games stretch vocabulary and spelling awareness.

Home Ideas:

- Make a rhyming chain: *'Cat, hat, bat, mat, fat, pat, rat, sat'*

FROM RHYME TO READING: HOW LANGUAGE PLAY BUILDS TO LITERACY

'Sing, ding, ping, wing, king, ring, ting-a ling'

'Phone, cone, moan, bone, loan, tone, zone'

You will notice that even though some of the words in the last list are not spelt the same way they still sound the same.

Play 'What's the Opposite?'

- For example: What is the opposite of *thick – thin*,

    What is the opposite of *wet-dry* and so on.

Play 'Name That Sound'

- For example: *What makes a whooshing noise?*

    What makes SSSS sound?

Games for Sequencing and Memory

5. 'What's Next?'

This game teaches sequencing and logical thinking.

How to Play:

Describe a common activity out of order

For example: *First you brush your teeth, then you put on your shoes, then you eat breakfast. Is that right?* . Let your child correct the order.

CHAPTER 8: LET'S PLAY LANGUAGE GAMES

Tip:

Create a 'routine puzzle' where they draw or arrange steps of a daily activity like getting ready for bed.

6. 'Follow the Instructions'

This simple listening game helps with comprehension and recall.

Example Prompts:

- *'Clap twice, spin around, then touch your toes.'*

- Add storytelling: *'Pretend you're a robot who can only follow exact commands!'*

'Let's go on a Sound Walk'

This is a good one for occasions when you have to walk somewhere and your child is reluctant or bored.

- As you walk through the mall, or shopping centre say *'Listen, what sounds can you hear?'* If your child shrugs or does not answer, say *'Can you hear footsteps?'* or *'Can you hear the coffee machine?' 'What else can you hear?'*

- If you are walking in the park, say *'Listen can you hear the kookaburra?'* or Can you hear a dog barking? *'What else can you hear?'*

- If you want to make it into imaginative play you could say *'Can you hear grandma mixing your favourite biscuit dough?'* or *'Can you hear what Daddy is doing right now?'*

Make It a Part of Everyday Life

Language games don't need to be formal or scheduled. They can happen in the car, at the dinner table, or while walking through the park. When we were driving through the country-side we used to ask the children to look for a white horse or a black dog. In the suburbs it could be who sees the first white fence, or a ginger cat or a person wearing a blue coat. If there is a choice of things to see, the child needs to repeat the whole sentence. For Example *'I can see/saw a white horse'*, or *'There is a lady with a yellow dress'*.

Try:

- Naming everything you see on a walk.

- Playing 'What rhymes with…?' during bath time. What rhymes with soap? (Pope, mope, dope, cope); What rhymes with sink? (wink, link, pink, mink, kink). It doesn't matter if your child makes up some words, so long as they rhyme. For example, for soap – boap, foap; or for sink – bink, hink.

- Asking silly questions at dinner *'Would you rather be… a lion or a tiger?'; 'Would you rather… pat a horse or a cat?'. 'Would you rather… grow a tail or a horn?'* follow their answer with the question *'Why?'* or *'What is better about your choice?'* or *'How would your life change ?'*

Summary: Your Role as a Language Coach

As a parent, your daily interactions have a lasting impact on your child's language development. By making language playful, accessible, and meaningful, you help them grow into confident communicators.

CHAPTER 8: LET'S PLAY LANGUAGE GAMES

Key Takeaways:

- Language games build essential skills through fun and connection.

- Use everyday moments to spark word play and storytelling.

- Adapt games to your child's age, interests, and attention span.

- Praise effort, not perfection—encouragement keeps them engaged.

Remember: The goal is not just to teach words—it's to create joyful conversations that make your child feel heard and empowered.

CHAPTER 9

LET'S READ TOGETHER

Reading aloud to your child is one of the most effective ways to expose them to language and literacy. Choose age-appropriate books with vibrant illustrations and engaging stories. Take the time to discuss the characters, settings, and events in fairy stories and other fiction books. When you use non-fiction/fact books explain unusual words and concepts and encourage your child to ask questions and share their thoughts. This practice helps develop vocabulary, comprehension skills, and a love for reading, another important factor in growing readers.

Before we go on to look at how to choose good books and the best ways to read to your child think about **everything you have read today**. When I did this exercise with my university students, we generated a long list of things they had read. Most of them had not really thought about the fact that they were reading. In your list did you include the time on the digital clock, the TV ads that had written words, the banner scrolling along the bottom of the TV news presentation, Stop signs, street names, advertisements on buildings, a recipe and so on. We read all day long. Think about what you can share with your child. Your child probably can already recognise the Stop sign. Find other signs in the environment that your child recognises. Recognising signs such as the MacDonald arches or the Coca-Cola logo is one of the first stages in early reading.

What can we Read Aloud?

Not only story books can be included in our read aloud material-

1. Alphabet books
2. Factual books.
3. Poetry
4. Comics
5. Magazines
6. Recipes
7. Pamphlets
8. Billboards
9. TV ads
10. Skywriting

How to Choose a Good Book to Read Aloud

Reading aloud to preschool children is one of the most important and enjoyable things you can do to support their early development. But with so many books on the shelves, how do you choose one that truly engages your child and supports their growth? Here are some tips for selecting quality books that are both fun and meaningful:

1. Start with Your Child's Interests

Choose books that reflect your child's passions—whether it's dinosaurs, fairies, trucks, or their favourite animals. When a story aligns with something your child already loves, they're more likely to be curious, engaged, and eager to listen. For example, if your child adores dogs, a story with a canine hero is likely to captivate their attention.

2. Look for Strong Picture Support

A well-designed picture book uses illustrations that enhance and support the text. The images not only match the story but often add extra detail and emotion that words alone may not express. Books like *The Very Hungry Caterpillar* by Eric Carle use simple but vibrant artwork to help children follow along. In this story, the caterpillar's journey is presented in clear, sequenced steps, leading to a satisfying and uplifting conclusion.

3. Choose Books with Rhyme or Rhythm

Younger children respond beautifully to stories told in rhyme or with a rhythmic pattern. The musicality of the language makes the book more engaging and easier to remember. Books like *We're Going on a Bear Hunt* by Michael Rosen or *Brown Bear, Brown Bear, What Do You See?* by Bill Martin Jr. and Eric Carle are beloved because of their repetitive, lyrical nature that begs to be read aloud.

4. Repetition is Key

Children thrive on repetition. Books with recurring phrases or repeated story patterns invite children to join in the storytelling. They learn to anticipate what comes next and feel empowered when they can 'read' along. Think of *The Very Busy Spider* by Eric Carle or *Each Peach Pear Plum* by Janet and Allan Ahlberg—books where children can quickly start to predict and participate.

5. Keep Text Simple and Manageable

For preschool-aged children, look for books that have only a small amount of text per page. One to two sentences are ideal for toddlers, while slightly older preschoolers might enjoy one or two short paragraphs. This allows children to focus on the story without feeling overwhelmed and gives you time to explore the pictures together.

6. Choose Stories with a Problem and a Resolution

Stories that feature a clear problem, challenge, or dilemma—and then work toward a satisfying resolution—mirror the way children make sense of their world. Books like *Who Sank the Boat?* by Pamela Allen present a simple problem that unfolds logically, with humour and insight, helping children learn about cause and effect.

7. Look for Emotional Learning

Books can be a gentle way to help children explore their emotions. Choose stories where characters experience feelings they can relate to—like sadness, jealousy, excitement, or frustration—and learn to understand or express those feelings. In *Wilfrid Gordon McDonald Partridge* by Mem Fox, the young hero learns about memory and emotions in a touching and relatable way.

8. Support Social Skills Development

Good books often include opportunities for children to learn about friendship, kindness, and cooperation. Stories where characters model polite behaviour, help others, or learn to share are not only enjoyable but also deeply educational. Books like *The Rainbow Fish* by Marcus Pfister or *Llama Llama Time to Share* by Anna Dewdney show young children how to navigate social situations.

9. Encourage Curiosity About the World

Some books help children explore the world around them—whether it's learning about animals, seasons, food, or different cultures. These stories expand a child's understanding and vocabulary. Look for books that gently introduce new ideas while keeping the tone light and playful. Titles like *From Head to Toe* by Eric Carle or *Handa's Surprise* by Eileen Browne can spark rich conversations and questions.

10. Ensure the Book is Age-Appropriate

Always consider whether the book is suitable for your child's age and developmental stage. Too many words, complex themes, or scary images can turn story-time into a struggle. Trust your instincts—you know your child best. Following, you'll find a curated list of classic and contemporary favourites that are perfect for preschoolers.

Classic and Much-Loved Books for Preschoolers

Below is a list of timeless stories that have stood the test of time and are treasured by generations of families. These books are ideal for reading aloud and are widely available at libraries and bookstores.

Picture Book Classics

- *The Very Hungry Caterpillar* by Eric Carle
  A gentle introduction to days of the week, numbers, and transformation. Also by Eric Carle, *The Very Busy Spider* and the *Very Lonely Firefly.*

- *Goodnight Moon* by Margaret Wise Brown
  A calming bedtime ritual book, perfect for winding down the day.

- *Where the Wild Things Are* by Maurice Sendak
  Explores imagination, emotions, and the comfort of coming home.

- *Possum Magic* by Mem Fox
  The story that explores protection, facing fears and includes the names of food and Australian cities. Also by Mem Fox are: *Shoes from Grandpa; Where is the Green Sheep; Koala Lou; Hattie and the Fox;* and *Time for Bed.*

- *Dear Zoo* by Rod Campbell
  Lift-the-flap fun with animals and repetitive structure. A similar book by him is *Noisy Farm.*

- *Owl Babies* by Martin Waddell
  A reassuring story about separation anxiety and the return of a parent.

- *The Snowy Day* by Ezra Jack Keats
  A simple, joyful exploration of a snowy urban day.

Picture Books that Teach Emotional and Social Understanding

- *Wilfrid Gordon McDonald Partridge* by Mem Fox
  A heartfelt exploration of memory and connection between generations.

- *The Rainbow Fish* by Marcus Pfister
  A shimmering story about the value of sharing and friendship.

- *Llama Llama Time to Share* by Anna Dewdney
  Gentle lessons about cooperation and playing together.

- *Giraffes Can't Dance* by Giles Andreae
  A celebration of individuality, self-expression, and perseverance.

- *Tucking Mummy In* by Morag Loh.
  A delightful story of understanding and role reversal.

- *Oi! Get off our Train* by John Burningham.
  This book uses animals to encourage inclusion and acceptance of people who are different.

- *The Very Bad Bunny* by Marilyn Sadler

A story about the choices we make and consequences

- *Harold and the Purple Crayon* by Crockett Johnson
  Another story about choices and includes colours

- *The Pokey Little Puppy* by Janette Lowrey. A Little Golden Book. A delightful tale of siblings, exploring the world around you and learning about rules. Some of the Little golden books are worth finding, This was my favourite.

Books About the Wider World

- *Handa's Surprise* by Eileen Browne
  Introduces fruits, animals, and cultural life in Kenya.

- *From Head to Toe* by Eric Carle
  Encourages movement and body awareness through interactive prompts.

- *We're Going on a Bear Hunt* by Michael Rosen
  A rhythmic, adventurous journey through different landscapes.

- *The Wonder Thing* by Libby Hathorn. A book with beautiful illustrations which encourages children to guess what the wonder thing is, while viewing many different cultures and countries.

- *Alexander's Outing* by Pamela Allen
  Alexander explores his local environment. *I wish I had a Pirate Suit,* is another by Pamela Allen.

Books that have a strong rhyming element.

- *The Cat in the Hat; Green Eggs and Ham* by Doctor Seuss

CHAPTER 9: LET'S READ TOGETHER

- *Brown Bear, Brown Bear, What Do You See?* by Bill Martin Jr. & Eric Carle
  A rhythmic classic that introduces colours and animals.

- *Room on the Broom* by Julia Donaldson & Axel Scheffler
  A fun, rhyming adventure about a witch and her animal friends.

- *The Gruffalo* by Julia Donaldson & Axel Scheffler
  A clever rhyming tale of a mouse outsmarting predators.

- *Chicka Chicka Boom Boom* by Bill Martin Jr. & John Archambault
  A lively alphabet rhyme that makes learning letters exciting.

- *We're Going on a Bear Hunt* by Michael Rosen & Helen Oxenbury
  A rhythmic, repetitive adventure that encourages interaction.

- *Giraffes Can't Dance* by Giles Andreae & Guy Parker-Rees
  An uplifting, rhyming story about embracing uniqueness.

- *Handa's Surprise* by Eileen Browne
  A rhythmic story that teaches about fruits and animals in a vibrant African setting.

- *The Wonky Donkey* by Craig Smith & Katz Cowley
  A hilarious, cumulative rhyme full of silly fun.

- *Each Peach Pear Plum* by Janet and Allan Ahlberg –
  A fun, rhyming 'I spy' book that encourages observational skills.

- *The Gingerbread Man* An American folk tale with the catchy phrase 'Run, run as fast as you can, you can't catch me I'm the gingerbread man.'

- *Shoes from Grandpa* by Mem Fox. A delightful tale in which the little girl receives different items of clothing that go with the shoes from Grandpa.

  This following are all rhyming books, so look out for them in the library. These are quite small books and they are a little bit quirky, but they might engage your child

- *The Croc put on a Sock and other Reading Rhymes* by Andrew Davies.

  In the same series are: *The Cat sat on the Mat, The Chick sat on the Brick,* and *The Newt put on a Suit.*

Book Selection Checklist for Parents

When you're standing in front of a shelf full of books (or scrolling through an online bookstore), use this quick checklist to guide your choices:

☑ Is the book **aligned with my child's interests** (e.g., animals, vehicles, food, feelings)?

☑ Do the **pictures support and enhance the story**, encouraging discussion and exploration?

☑ Does the book have **rhyme, rhythm, or repetition** that will engage my child's ear and memory?

☑ Is the **text short and manageable** (1–2 sentences per page for toddlers; short paragraphs for older preschoolers)?

☑ Does the story have a **clear structure** (a beginning, middle, and satisfying end)?

☑ Does it include a **problem and solution** that mirrors real-life challenges for young children?

☑ Will it help my child explore **emotions, social skills, or new ideas** in a safe and age-appropriate way?

☑ Is the **language rich and playful**, exposing my child to new words and expressions?

☑ Can I see us **reading it again and again** with pleasure?

☑ Has the book won an **award**?

☑ Has the book been **shortlisted** by the Australian Children's Book Council?

Choosing the Best Books

Libraries and Book Councils in various countries annually select the best children's books to receive awards. As I am writing in the Australian context, I will give you details about the winning Australian books (www.cbca.org.au). If you are interested in other countries' awards go to the following websites:

Canada: www.bookcentre.ca/pages/ccbc-book-awards

NZ: www.nzbookawards.nz

UK: www.fcbg.org.uk/childrens-book-award

USA: www.nypl.org/blog

Each year, the Australian Children's Book Council selects the best children's books, that have been published that year, in Australia, to receive an award as the 'Book of the Year'. They first select what they call 'notables' and from those, shortlist the best of the group before choosing the **Book of the Year** in each category.

The website information about the 2025 entries indicates:

> *We received 730 entries for 15 expert judges to assess in this year's awards. The notables showcases the work of 122 books, representing 31 publishers, 114 writers and 79 illustrators. These categories reflect the breadth of children's literature written by Australians. They also reflect our aim to promote quality reading for young Australians of a wide age-range and reader ability.*

It is a good idea to have a look at the books that were shortlisted and have won *Book of the Year* awards. You will find them in book shops, and they can be identified easily, as they will have a sticker on them that says either they were shortlisted or that they have won the book award. Below are the shortlisted books. Winners are starred.

The 2025 Australian *Book of the Year* shortlist for Early Childhood books is:

- ***Don't Worry, Felix*** by Yohann Devezy & Katharine Alice, illustrated by Zoe Bennett (New Frontier Publishing)

- ***Everything You Ever Wanted to Know About the Tooth Fairy (And Some Things You Didn't)*** by Briony Stewart (Lothian Children's Books)

CHAPTER 9: LET'S READ TOGETHER

- *How to Move a Zoo* by Kate Simpson, illustrated by Owen Swan (A&U Books for Children and Young Adults)

- *One Little Dung Beetle* by Rhiân Williams, illustrated by Heather Potter & Mark Jackson (Wild Dog Books)

- *Spiro* by Anna McGregor (Scribble)

- *The Wobbly Bike* by Darren McCallum, illustrated by Craig Smith (Walker Books Australia) **Winner*

The 2025 Australian *Book of the Year* shortlist for Children's Picture Books is:

- *Afloat* by Freya Blackwood, text by Kirli Saunders (Little Hare)

- *The Garden of Broken Things* by Freya Blackwood (HarperCollins AU)

- *A Leaf Called Greaf* by Kelly Canby (Fremantle Press)

- *These Long-Loved Things* by Ronojoy Ghosh, text by Josh Pyke (Scholastic Australia)

- *The Truck Cat* by Danny Snell, text by Deborah Frenkel (Bright Light) **Winner*

- *We Live in a Bus* by Dave Petzold (Thames & Hudson Australia)

The Shortlist for the Eve Pownall Award, the award for Australian Children's Non-Fiction books

- *Design & Building on Country* (Alison Page & Paul Memmott, illus by Blak Douglas, Thames & Hudson)

- ***Always Was, Always Will Be*** (Aunty Fay Muir & Sue Lawson, Magabala) **Winner

- ***Flora: Australia's Most Curious Plants*** (Tania McCartney, NLA)

- ***I Am a Magpie, I Am a Currawong*** (Bridget Farmer, Black Cockatoo Books)

- ***Making the Shrine: Stories from Victoria's War Memorial*** (Laura J Carroll, The Crossley Press)

- ***South with the Seabirds*** (Jess McGeachin, A&U Children's)

How to read to your child.

Now that together you have chosen a well written book that is of interest and age appropriate for your child we need to think about how to go about the reading.

- ***Sit side by side.*** The most important thing to remember when reading aloud with your child is to sit next to each other, so your child can see the words and pictures in the book. I remember the first time my daughter asked her father to read her a story. He was sitting in his favourite comfy chair and she sat on the pouffe in front of him. He opened the book and began reading, so all my daughter could see was the cover. I did not want to interrupt, but knew she would not last long, just listening, without seeing the pictures. Soon she was crawling off her seat and rolling on the floor. The reading stopped and he said 'Well that was a waste of time'. I then suggested that they sit side by side so she could see the pictures, which produced a much more satisfying outcome for both of them.

- **Use expression.** It might feel a little strange at first, but using an expressive voice and sound effects can captivate your child's attention and make the story more exciting. *(For Example: Using a deep voice for a bear character, or a high squeaky voice for a mouse.)*

- **Turning the page.** When you turn the page, wait for your child to look at the pictures before you read the words. This encourages them to anticipate what the words might be and helps them to focus on the words when you read them. If you turn the page and immediately read the words, the child will be focussing on the pictures rather than the words and may miss some of the story.

- **Mid-way through the story.** Before you turn a page, in the middle of the story, you can ask 'I wonder what will happen next?' Even if the child does not answer it will encourage them to think about possible things that might happen.

- **At the end of the story.** After you turn the final page, make a comment, such as 'I liked the part when they got into the boat to start the adventure. Which part did you like best?' Or you could each find your favourite picture and say why.

- **Talk about the characters.** You could ask: 'Why do you think the character made that choice?' What did the character learn in this story?

- **Talk about the message.** If the story has a strong theme, such as facing your fears, admitting you did something wrong, or the value of friends: You could introduce the notion of a deeper message to the story by making a statement such as: 'I thought that …(name the character) was very brave when she faced the (…). What do you think the message is for us? If your child can't name the message, you state it in the form, 'Do you think it might be......?' If the child agrees, that they get a feeling of understanding a deeper message. If they disagree, then ask what they think? All opinions are valid, so accept it by saying: 'It could be', or 'You may be right'. This will leave your child feeling satisfied that they understood the message and that you value their opinions.

I have found that my children had favourite that books that they wanted me to read to them over and over. I would not use all of the above suggestions every time I read to them. I would start with the simplest options. Then the next time I read the book to them I would ask a question that was a bit harder or more involved. This way each time you read the story they gain a little more understanding about the story, the characters and the message. If your child likes to have a different story every time you read together then use your judgement about what sort of questions to ask. This will depend on the age of your child, their level of interest in the story and whether or not you believe it is worth delving deeper into the meaning.

Happy Reading!

CHAPTER 10

LET'S SCRIBBLE, WRITE, TYPE AND DRAW!

Does your child have a colouring in book? Do they have pencils and paper? Do they have pens? Do they have paints? Most children love to make marks on paper or in books. Often it is just scribble, but once they get the idea that you can write things down, perhaps they see you writing a shopping list, maybe they could write their own shopping list with their squiggles. Whatever they pretend to do for writing, encourage them to do it as it is a good start for pre-school and school.

The Reading Writing Connection

Reading and writing today is almost completely intertwined. When children go to school it is difficult to separate the two skills, because of the advent of technology. Much of a child's early learning is done on iPads and computers, such that reading and writing seem to happen simultaneously. Handwriting may not be taught as a separate skill, as it used to be, when I went to school and when I first began teaching.

Is it Writing or Scribble?

Not all of life depends on technology, so any writing that your child wants to do, even pretend writing scribbles is fine. If they draw a picture, ask if they can you tell you about it. You could suggest giving the drawing a title. Help them think up a title and encourage them to write it at the top or bottom of the picture or you could print it at the top and read it to them. Don't worry if their title is just scribble so long as they can tell you what it says. This is making sure they understand that we can write something down and 'read' it back. A useful skill for school. If they know how to write any letters of the alphabet they might use them as part of their pretend writing. This also should be encouraged, as it is really helpful when they get to school and start to learn to read and write. If they want to learn how to form the letters correctly, you could buy some magnetic plastic letters to put on the fridge. Your child could copy them or perhaps you could write the letters, particularly the letters of their name. Write some letters down and encourage your child can trace over them. Make sure that the letters you print are not too small.

Chalk Drawings

If they have chalk sometimes it's fun for them to draw on the footpath if that's allowed. I know that during COVID, there were lots of chalk drawings on the footpaths near my home. Even when we were only allowed out for short periods of time we could see some inventive drawings and writing on footpaths and it brightened our day.

Chalk usually rubs off, or hoses off fairly easily, so you could make a little area in your yard for chalk drawing, or perhaps you've got a chalkboard. Most children love to draw on a chalkboard. Following a walk to the park, or a family outing, you could encourage your child to draw something about the outing on the chalkboard. You could ask them to write a title for their drawing, or to write the names of the things they have drawn. Then once again ask them to read their writing to you. They can be quite inventive in their reading.

Using Technology to read and write

I mentioned using digital tools such as iPads or computers or even phones. If you have an old computer or iPad encourage your children to get on and type. It does not matter if what they type to begin with is a jumble of letters. You might then point to one or two of the keys and tell them the name of the letter. This will help them begin to learn some of the letter names. See if they can pick out the first letter of their name. If they are already at pre-school they may be able to pick out their whole name. Then maybe they could type *mum* or *dad* or the name of your dog or your cat. It is all very helpful for when they get to school and for their developing literacy and their ability with typing on computers and iPads.

Most young children these days know their way around a mobile phone and can navigate simple games. Have you thought about using some educational apps or audiobooks? There are some language learning platforms and online storytelling apps which young children can watch or access. For example, they might watch an animated story on *YouTube Kids.*

Monitoring Screen Time

As a parent, you need to monitor the screen time that your children are having, because a lot of research has shown that a small amount of screen time, particularly for educational purposes is beneficial, but when it's just used as child minding it is detrimental. Don't worry, we are all guilty of using technology to gain some adult time, especially when you want to get dinner ready. We have all said: 'Yes go and watch the cartoons for half an hour'. I don't think there's anything wrong with that, but if it's for extended periods of time then it has tends to isolate the child from normal conversations and from family interactions.

A Parents' Role

Parents have a vital role in fostering language development in their preschool children. By creating a language-rich environment, reading aloud, expanding vocabulary, singing songs, engaging in conversation, playing language games, utilizing technology wisely, providing multilingual experiences if you speak other languages at home, and being language models, parents can significantly enhance their child's language skills. Building language skills helps to grow readers, so that when your child starts school they are well prepared for literacy.

Summary: Remember that each child is unique, so adapt these ideas to suit your child's individual needs, strengths, and interests. By investing time and effort during these early years, you can unlock their child's potential and set them on a path to lifelong learning.

CHAPTER 11

LET'S GET READY FOR KINDY

How do you know that your child is ready for kindy? Some schools now have pre-kindergarten and three-year-old kindergarten, so those children are very young when they start. Frequently, such young children have not been away from their parents for any length of time, so it can be a big wrench for them. While some children are happy to leave their parent, others take some time. Often schools are quite happy for parents or caregivers to stay for a little while until the child is settled.

Helping Out at Kindy

Luckily, most kindergartens welcome parents as parent helpers. One of my sons really did not want to leave me and go to Kindy, so on his first day I signed up for as many parent helper sessions as I possibly could. After the first couple of sessions, he didn't care whether I was there or not, but I had already signed up so I had to do all of my parent duty days. It was fortunate that I was not working at the time, and I enjoyed doing it, even though I was not very good at sorting muddled up jigsaw pieces and putting them together correctly.

Adapting to Change and Learning New Things

Often even the most reluctant children get used to the new structure and enjoy being with other children. It does take some children a little while to adapt, so don't worry if your child is reluctant to let go of your hand in the beginning.

What sorts of things do children need to learn or be able to do at Kindy, so that they will be happy and get on with the other children? We know about knowing how to sit down and have their snack, being able to go to the toilet by themselves, or with only a little help with clothing.

Other important traits children need to learn at Kindy are the ability to:

- interact with other students,
- interact with teachers and adult helpers,
- understand and follow directions,
- be able to take turns,
- focus on a single activity for an extended period of time,
- cope with disappointment and frustration,

Pre-Literacy Skills

What is going to help your child with the pre-literacy skills that are taught at Kindergarten? The following will help:

- familiarity with books,
- the ability to sit still and listen to a story being read,
- familiarity with one or two nursery rhymes,
- being able to hold a pencil or crayon and scribble for prewriting skills,

- being able to draw, even if nothing is recognisable to us,

- being able to use their words to communicate.

In addition to these items, it is useful if your child has some concept of number. For example, if they can do a little bit of counting and recognising some numbers that's always very helpful.

Summary: If you have been reading to your child during the day or at bed time, and singing a few nursery rhymes then your child is on the way to a successful pre-literacy experience at Kindergarten. If they can recognise their own name that is an added bonus, although it might be a bit much for a three year old. If you have been following some of the activities in this book, then your child will find many of the activities at Kindy are somewhat familiar. The additional pre-literacy activities at Kindergarten are designed to fully prepare your child for reading once they start school. If your child has finished Kindergarten and is getting ready for big school, then read on, the final chapter covers getting ready for school.

CHAPTER 12

LET'S START SCHOOL!

In this final section we're going to have a look at what sorts of things are absolutely optimum for your child when they are heading off to school. In particular, we will be thinking about language and literacy learning, and what is going to help your child at school. Let us make of list and see how many you can tick off, when you think about your child.

Does your child,

- show some idea of real-world knowledge and understand a range of different topics? I am sure your child understands their home and who the members of your own home are. They probably know members of your extended family, such as grandparents, aunts, uncles and cousins. They may also know the members of the kindergarten community, if they attended one. ☑

- understand something about different environments? For example, there's the home environment, there is also a community, a shopping centre, the library, the park or the bush and the church or community centre. ☑

- know about different foods that we eat and where they come from? Many young children think that food comes from the supermarket, but do not understand that a lot is grown on farms and that other foods are made in factories from other ingredients. ☑

- understand something about which clothes we wear in different seasons of the year? ☑

The areas mentioned above, are all key learning areas. Hopefully you were able to tick off most if not all of the above items. It is beneficial if your child has developed an understanding of a range of these different areas, because a lot of the books that they will read, once they get to school, will focus on things that a child is likely to know about, such as home and family and their environment.

We have talked about that important background knowledge that teachers can build on in the first days of school. Your child will have at least one story read to them each day at school, alongside gradually learning to read themselves.

Does your child,

- have some understanding about who is doing what in the books that you read to them? This means they understand who a particular character is, whether it's an animal or a person and what he or she is doing? ☐

- have an understanding what happens in the beginning, the middle and the end of a story? ☐

- hear and say everyday words? Do they have a bank of a lot of words that they can say, but also understand some uncommon words that they don't say yet? ☐

- learn a number of nursery rhymes at Kindy, from TV or from books? Can they recite a few rhymes? ☐

- know that some words can rhyme? Can they say a rhyming word if given a different word? ☐

The Benefits of Learning about Rhyme

Understanding that words can rhyme is a really important concept for children to understand as they start to learn about the letters of the alphabet and the sounds that they each make. Your child might already know some of the alphabet. They might be able to sing the alphabet song.. Maybe they know how to clap the syllables in their name or they might know how to sound out their name.

Does your child,

- know that the funny squiggles on a page in a book (the text) is what contains the meaning? ☐

  NB: When we read a story to a little child, they usually look at the pictures, but do they know that the black squiggles mean anything? It is quite an important concept for them to grasp in order for them to learn how to read. If they don't get it, they just keep looking at the pictures and then guess the meaning.

Letters and Sounds

Does your child,

- recognise their own name and begin to be able to write it? That's a good start. ☐

- write a few other words or use plastic letters on the fridge to make some words? ☐

That's a good way of helping them to identify that there are letters, and the letters make up words. Once they get to school, one of the first things they have to learn is what's called the alphabetic principle. The alphabetic principle basically says that words are made up of letters, that each letter has its own sound, and that different letters can be put together to make different sounds. For example the letter 'A' says 'a' as in 'hat' in lots of words, but sometimes it goes together with other letters like an 'R' which makes a new sound: 'ar' as in 'car'.

You don't have to teach your child these things. If your child can recite some nursery rhymes and can print some of the letters of their own name they are their well on the way to understanding that alphabetic principle.

Understanding Stories

Does your child understand the stories you read to them? When your child begins to read for themselves they not only have to get the words off the page, they need to understand the meaning. That is what we call reading comprehension.

- How do you know that your child has understood the story that you've read to them? Perhaps you could ask them what the story was about, or what their favourite part was. Sometimes young children get a completely muddled idea of what the story is about. If that happens, you could ask questions to help them to see that there's another possible interpretation of the story. Use questions that begin like this:

Do you think that maybe ....? Is it possible that....? This way you are not telling the child that they are wrong but offering another perspective.

- How do you know that your child's vocabulary is sufficient to understand a range of words that are found in children's books?

Vocabulary Development

I've talked about vocabulary development before. It is important that your child has a reasonably wide vocabulary. Can they understand more words than they can say? That is the difference between their expressive vocabulary, which are the words that they can say, and their receptive vocabulary which are the words that they understand, but they don't actually use. Has your child been exposed to some uncommon words? It is not the number of words they know that is most import, but the variety.

Learning Teamwork

Finally, a good social skill for them to begin to develop before going to school is teamwork. If they have been to Kindy, or they have been in playgroups they have learned how to cooperate with other children in a group and share toys. You might be thinking, how is this related to reading. Once they get to school they will usually be put into little groups for reading, and sometimes they have to read the same story, talk to each other about it, or explain things to the child next to them. Being used to talking and sharing with other children helps when it comes to doing that sort of activity.

Summary: We are at the end, and if you have followed some of the activities, rhymes and advice in this book, you can be confident that you have given your child a great start to their formal education at school. Be on the look out for the next book for parents of children in the first few years of school. My very best wishes for a happy start for you and your child on the next great adventure, *Going to School.*

Ready for School

ABOUT THE AUTHOR

Dr Marion Milton (Phd, M Ed, B Ed) was a teacher educator for over 20 years and worked at universities in Western Australia, New South Wales and Victoria. Prior to that she taught in primary, secondary and special schools. Her qualifications include a Master's degree in Teaching English as an additional language and a Doctorate that researched the psycholinguistic factors that impact on early reading.

As a University Professor, Dr Milton has been involved in many local and national research studies that focused on the learning and teaching of literacy in children and adults. Her areas of research included: Beginning Literacy, Literacy Difficulties and English as an Additional Language. Her findings are published widely in journals and books.

Her expertise is valued nationally and internationally. She has been an invited curriculum writer for beginning literacy education in government schools in Western Australia, and has conducted professional development for teachers, on effective literacy teaching strategies for students with literacy or learning difficulties. Most recently she has been a school reviewer for the Education Department of WA, Non-Government schools and Catholic Education WA.

Dr Milton has reviewed articles for *Education Science,* and *The Reading Teacher,* both international peer-reviewed journals, and was an invited member of the International Advisory Board for EDULEARN International Conferences.

Dr Milton is the mother of four grown children and lives in Western Australia.

www.ingramcontent.com/pod-product-compliance
Lightning Source LLC
Chambersburg PA
CBHW060406080526
44583CB00012B/483